Memorabilia

Poems from time to time

Walter Nash

First Published 2009

ISBN 9781899605-08-8

Beyond the Cloister Publications

74 Marina St Leonards-on-Sea TN38 0BJ England

To Helen —

always my lass,

alike in days of easy going or hard graft —

this book is dedicated

4

By the same author:

Poems

East West Risen
Feather Books 2002
Of Time and Small Islands
Beyond the Cloister 2006
In Good Faith— devotional poems 1997--2007
Feather Books 2007

On Language and Literature

The Language of Humour
Longman 1985
Rhetoric: the Wit of Persuasion
Blackwell 1989
Language in Popular Fiction
Routledge 1990
(with Ronald Carter) Seeing through Language
Blackwell 1990
An Uncommon Tongue—The Uses and Resources of English
Routledge 1992
Jargon, its Uses and Abuses
Blackwell 1993
Language and Creative Illusion
Longman 1998
A Departed Music: Old English Poetry
Anglo-Saxon Books 2006

Autobiography

For Old Times Sake: Childhood in the 1930's
Bright Pen (colophon of Authors Online) 2007

FOREWORD

The poems collected in this book all have to do with memory, in one way or other of the diverse nuances of that complex word: memory as remembrance, recall, reminiscence, recollection — ultimately as cognition, for this is an old man's book, and old men, I find, understand the world in the light of their memories.

Its first section, called "Early Days" is a record of childhood and youth in the 1930's and early 1940's. The second set, "Love and Friendship" are poems on personal relationships, failed or fulfilled. The third sequence, "Late News", is a view of contemporary life in the perspectives of age and — to borrow a phrase from Philip Larkin — "the only end of age".*

With one or two exceptions the poems were composed between 1998 and 2008. Several have been published, but in the present process of re-collection have undergone some revision. Among periodicals represented, with my acknowledgements, are *Acumen, The Interpreter's House, Pause, Poetry Church*, and the *Feather Books Poetry Series*; and in the U S A, the on-line magazines *Words on the Wind* and *Contemporary Rhyme.*

For encouragement generously given, I thank my editor, Hugh Hellicar, and would also wish to pay a recurrent debt of obligation to John Waddington-Feather, first editor to foster and publish any of my poetry. For the support I have drawn, in conversation or correspondence with friends and fellow poets, I am deeply grateful. First and last among my supporters is my wife Helen, "my lass", to whom this collection is happily dedicated.

Walter Nash
Acantilado de los Gigantes
Tenerife   2008

* The closing phrase of his poem "Dockery and Son"; *Collected Poems*, Marvell Press and Faber, London 1988 p.152

A DECLARATION

Come, poems, I'll be your fellow,
feel your own way
between the thorn and the rose,
be surly or mellow,
or madly gay,
whichever you choose, but follow
nobody else's nose

Pursue what path you will;
to everything there's a season,
in every purpose a time
for dancing, or drill,
a time for the murmur of reason
a time for the shrill
skirling insistence of rhyme.

Go sport with politicians
and popinjays, go mock
the powers above
with rants and inquisitions,
go scathe, go shock;
but then, musicians,
sing of the sweetness of love.

What else is to declare?
Nothing especially new,
beyond the happenstance
that governs everywhere
and lets a song ring true;
to this unoriginal air,
dance, my veterans, dance.

Contents

Early days

That which hath been is now: and
that which is to be hath already been;
and God requireth that which is past.

Ecclesiastes 3: 15

BEFOREHAND

When lesser breeds feared our imperial anger,
  and Britain ruled – so Rudyard Kipling sang –
in every patch and parish of the atlas,
  my father was a boy; I savour that
first decade of the twentieth century –
  a blond heat-haze, the faint recessive scent
of serge and muslin – and retrieve not only
  my father's boyhood, but – almost – my own.
How come this intuition of of a sharing,
  this prompting that persuades me I was *there*?
There, with his jersey and his coarse knee-breeches,
  the Norfolk jacket he assumed for each
visit to Sunday kin. It's anecdotal,
  this hindsight, I suppose; I have by rote
my father's boyish jokes, his songs, the feelings
  that drove him then; so memory reveals
the tales my parents told about their gaddings
  when mother was in service, and my dad
newly apprenticed as an engine-fitter.
  Those were the bandstand times, when streets were lit
with gas, and vaudevilles of bustling bodies
  flung jeers and laughter to the braying gods.
King Edward's manly phiz on massive pennies
  could get you – they would joke – such treasures then:
Lucifer matches, candles, plug tobacco,
  a quarter-ounce of yeast – and a farthing back.
A patriot time: dear Land of Hope and Glory,
  street parties, bunting, feasts: yet still the poor,
still in their always-withness, were in attendance,
  their stillness boding how it all might end.
See them in photographs, fixed in the long exposure,
  the barefoot urchins, pinafored lasses, rows
of gramps and grannums, looking patiently
  towards the camera: set in each tranquil face
a lost, submissive questioning of their Masters:
  What are we for? What shall we come to at last?
Well, this was the twentieth century. Surely, slowly
  as the shutter closed upon them, they would know.

AN OLD PHOTOGRAPH
("The Barrow-in-Furness Pals." 1915)

So there you are, boys, in your issue kit
posing, so clearly
pleased, cockahoop, though maybe embarrassed a bit
by the rub of the khaki cloth, the approximate fit —
it becomes you rarely,
so fairly, so queerly.

"Pals" you are called, together grown
to manhood but lately,
four and twenty men of a northern town,
unwilling to let the redfaced terraces down,
you joined up so lightly,
rejoicing so greatly.

And had you then no other delight?
Your pleasure, purely,
the music hall, a football match or a fight,
your giggly girls, and the chipper on Saturday night,
you'd miss them sorely,
presently, surely?

Could a working lad have honour in mind?
Instinct not solely
for comradeship and the simple love of his kind,
but his country's service following, trusting, blind,
in faithfulness lowly,
exalted, wholly?

Well, here you grin at the horror to come,
that spectre austerely
stalking at Loos, and the stricken fields of the Somme,
and all but two of you will never get home;
came death to parley
too freely, too early.

Note: The "Pals" were battalions of volunteers, recruited in the period
1914-1916 before conscription was introduced. Men from the same district
or town, sometimes from the same block of streets, joined up together,
trained together, went to France together and mostly died together. Of the
two survivors in the photograph, which my mother treasured, one was her
brother Tom. The other was "invalided out", after the Somme, certified
insane.

WITH PUNS AND PAPER AEROPLANES

With puns and paper aeroplanes
my father made his children smile,
with juggling tricks and old refrains
from vaudeville, long out of style

like jokes that surely had their day
when Joe Grimaldi plied his craft;
no matter; we laughed, anyway;
he was our dad – of course we laughed.

He tested us with spelling bees
and tried to teach us how to swim;
we did our childish best to please,
of course; the world grew up in him.

Dickens he loved, and Carroll next,
and sometimes, in his solemn vein
spoke sheer Micawber, till his text
betrayed him, and he laughed again.

Was least alone when most apart
at the piano, playing through
familiar numbers that his heart
put in his hands – *Ombra mai fú*

or *Träumerei,* then, as he spelt
the shape of the melodic line
his face grew still, as though he felt
the healing touch of a divine

invading presence in the airs
Handel or Robert Schumann sent
down the hard labour of the years
in sweet affirming testament

that life is more than bed and work,
that there's an action of the soul
against the mocking shades that lurk
between a night shift and the dole.

This legacy my father left:
out of the rubble of brave lives
discarded, overborne, bereft,
something is rescued. Love survives

THE LAST PITCH OF THE STAIR

In the days of candlelight
at the last pitch of the stair
was the place at bedtime every night
where I balked and resisted, bawling in fright,
because the devils were there.

Where the old bead-curtain hung
I felt them touch my head.
I thought they fingered my ljps and tongue,
and sightless upon my eyelids swung
the malevolent undead.

To poultice my alarm
and make the devils go,
sister would chant some powerful charm
like "Old Macdonald had a farm"
or "One man went to mow."

Songs are healers, and some
have the merit of answered prayer;
then I pray God send me tunes to hum
or verses to make, when I shall come
to the last pitch of the stair.

TEMPERATE CLIMATE (1930)

There were women always ready
to weep or throw a punch,
sponges of moist affection,
oceans of breaking passion,
such an impetuous bunch,

taking it out on the coalman,
or laughing with her next door,
the shapes of their broken cloudscape
from floor-up I remember
as viewed at the age of four.

The men were morosely stubbled:
teeth clenched on pipestems, they sat,
saying "aye, appen", and looking
quite small in the lee of ladies
full-figured, or *stout*, (never fat),

before slipping away to the privy
to read the News hung on the nail,
and brood on the sad mischances
of a team at the foot of the table,
or a horse that could only fail.

These presences made the weathers
that whispered around me then
in my old north country childhood:
a climate of warm wet women
with outbreaks of cool dry men

A LINE HELD
(1933-5: in the Depression)

They
would sit of a night in the back room
where the fire made merry behind its bars
and the gas mantle hissed –
comfortable pair,

he
stockstill in Goldsmith or sunk in Dickens,
nods recognition to a stray thought,
fitfully easing his backside
on ancient springs,

she
filletting with satiric eye
cuts of The Lancashire Evening Post,
with occasional pause to rejoice
over gossips routed,

soon
has to put up his "snap" for the morning -
bread and cheese in the flat tin box,
tea in a paper screw
(give us this day),

and the "maid" -
clothes horse – waits, with tomorrow's shirt
warming for half-past five o'clock;
"tha's work to go to" – the word
calls him to bed,

while the fire
banked up and guarded in the grate,
blurts lapping syllables of light,
and mantel clock ticks out
a regular tale

whose plot
will never turn on victory won,
only on common steadfastness,
a stand for decency,
a line held.

NORTHERN WASHDAY
(1930s)

Monday was always washday, unless it rained,
and for that we had a spell: rain, go away,
we sang, rain go away and come again
another washing day; and it often did.

For my mother, a day of Herculean labours: fill
the great copper vat in the wash-house with water, light
the fire beneath (fetching paper and sticks and coals);
then in with the week's washing, in with sheets
and shirts and camisoles, long johns, singlets, bloomers,
in with the flannel nighties and pyjamas,
in with the coverlets and the bolster cases,
writhing and rolling in the steaming flood,
down with them, then, harry them, push them deeper,
dollylegs twisting, bell of the posser plunging,
then up with the washboard and the scrubbing brush,
and then to the rinsing, and then to the wringing by hand,
wrist moving counter to wrist, the biceps tense,
the stomach taut with the effort, and so to the mangle
with its great cast-iron wheel and heavy rollers,
double sheets muscled through, put to the question,
squeezed till the tears run down to the wash-house floor.
My mother's hair is awry, her face is scarlet,
sweat blinds her, breath's a whistle in her throat;
but all's not done yet: load the clothes in a basket
and out to the back street where her line is hoisted
on timber props; she grips the pegs in her mouth
as garment by garment the clothes go up to dry
(the sheets are a trouble, the coverlets even worse
to double over the line; she's five feet small,
and it's hard wrestling with a wayward load).
But done at last, there's time to find herself
and let the clenching springs of work unwind.
She leans against the backstreet wall, her arms
folded across her chest, the one knee flexed,
her head bowed down, as though in meditation.

So often, as a boy, I saw her thus;
and now, in age, recall her old reproof
when she was fretted, work-worn and beset
with graceless children: "You don't know you're born".

OLDER NOW

Older now than my father was on that day
when the dark got into his head, and he fell on the landing, and lay
till the ambulancemen lifted him, and he died,
older now,
I look up to him still, I talk to him in my sleep,
craving his counsel, comfort, wisdom; from that deep
he considers me gravely, puzzlefaced, dark-eyed -
older now,

But never so young as my mother, all her long years,
who laughed till the laughter choked and spilled into helpless tears
and her blind eye joined in a twinkling with the sound –
never so young.
I have the glimpse of her everywhere, I meet
the shape of her, glad among neighbours in the street,
wherever there´s life and gossip afoot, she´s found –
ever so young

GRANDPARENTS

Then what should I say of them, the Old Folk?
Remote as Romans all my lifetime ago.

They were self-reliant.
They never phoned their broker, or lobbied their MP
Or ever wrote to *The Times.*

They did not talk about books as if they had read them.
He had his *Pink 'Un,* she *The Holy Bible.*
Each plumbed the meaning of each.

They would have found curious the importunate whining
Of our multistockoptional
Tax-rebating
Desirable property owning, upgrading, dieting,
Shareholding, exercising, self-absorbed and absorbent,
Relentlessly middleclassnattering
State.

They had regard for their neighbours, respect for themselves.

They made the most of it,
That "station in life to which they had been called"
With love, courage, resourcefulness, humour; even in despair
They had their grandeur.

At length they moved to a little green mound in the graveyard,
Unmarked – but the poor could rarely afford a marker –
Numbered – but now the whereabouts are lost.

It makes no matter – for sure, they have been called
To a grander station on a better line.

LITTLE MISS MURRAY
(a street preacher)

For little Miss Murray, so quaint
in her black straw bonnet and shawl,
who handed sweets around
when my world was at ten to seven;
for the memory of that saint
in sneakers, *Praise, my soul
the King of Heaven.*

With winegums and lemondrops
she preached in the old back street
where we hunkered on steps, or the ground
while she spoke of our friend, a King
whose care for us never stops,
and told us, *To His feet
thy tribute bring.*

In remembrances of the past
a hidden code is revealed,
a singular child is found,
a forgotten gift is given;
heart, may we hope at last
we shall be *Ransomed, healed,
restored, forgiven?*

Rejoice, my soul, in that friend,
though my world is at half-past three,
and my doubts and fears abound;
if a child remembered may bring
assurance that all will end
in sweetness, *Who like thee
His praise should sing*?

VAL CUMBERBATCH
(Rugby League, 1930s)

Val Cumberbatch running, to win the match,
breaking away on the wing, shaking
one tackle off, then two, and their full back
coming too late to forestall the try in the corner -

adept, rapt, he moves, in arrogant flight
swooping, swerving, on elegant legs loping,
the stands go silly, but he, as in a stillness,
nearing yet barely hearing the crowd's cheering,

moves, with a scholar's gravity, through groves
of contemplation towards a temple of praise
where anthems disrupt his study, and his body
lies prone and gasping among the exultations -

this I remember from my boyhood years,
remember it now in the trance of a halting sentence,
remember the power of it, the grace, the composure
humbly recall, as I stumble into verse.

LONDON, MIDLAND & SCOTTISH
(1938-9)

Praise we the power of the proud locomotive,
cheerfully chugging through holiday England
sweeping through stations with magical messages –
"Stephens' Ink", "Vimto", "Palethorpe's Sausages" -
bearing us off into Punch and Judydom,
jaunting us into a holiday world.

Bless we the spell of the Saturday cinema,
magical matinee, penny-for-dreamtime,
fighting for France with fabulous swordsmen,
riding the range with musical horsemen,
Laurel and Hardy, Chaplin and Keaton,
fencing us into a funny old world.

Mourn we the Jarrowmen, marching hungry,
adrift in the daze of the daylong counties,
trudging their trouble to faraway London,
doomed though the enterprise, dead the endeavour;
mourn we the ranks of the workless, forever
walking the roads of a hapless world.

Fear we the tread of the Fascist triumphant,
flags, poses, parades, goose-steps,
see in the headlines, hear on the wireless,
(But what's this to us? Let us only be warless),
turn up the sound, and listen to Hitler
preaching his peace to a terrified world.

Bear we the shame of the long appeasement,
Anschluss, Sudeten, corridored Danzig,
Czechoslovakia – Chamberlain pouting,
"A faraway country of which we know nothing",
the displaced folk of a bartered Europe
bearing the cross of a pacified world.

Mind we that morning in early September,
shock-still the air as the clock struck eleven,
women by many a wireless, weeping,
a grey voice: "...no such undertaking...
we are at war..."; then the sirens jeering,
braying the fall of Britannia's world.

THE CONSCRIPT
(1944)

My generation could talk about the War
   as if it were a stint in a bearable hell -
rationing, blackout, firewatch, nights in the shelter -
   it all comes back to us as funny and boring:
service life, even, could be a dusty joke;
   in every camp a lawyer and a jester,
the theatre of sergeants, the professed
   cowardice, acceptable as smoking.

Only when recollection touches those camps
   where lawyers could never plead, or sees war ramping
in places where the face of God was baneful
do silences expand, anguished and awkward,
   and words contrive the formal, stumbling talk
of a sonnet that tries to rhyme and cannot explain

HARD SHIPS
(R.N. training establishment: 1944)

et te sonantem plenius aureo
Alcaee, plectro dura navis
   Horace, Odes II, xiii

CPO Barker was, you might say, Old Navy;
thirty years in the Service, man and boy,
finished his twelve, signed on for a second twelve,
and now, in Hitler's war, serving a third,
teaching parade ground drill to sloppy recruits,
and filling them with dread and merriment.
There was Jutland in the the jet of his jaw, his voice
was glass and gravel as he told us tales
of how things were in days afore the war,
in the *pusser* Navy, not this present lot,
when ships was ships and men was iron men.
"Hardships?" he'd growl. "Ha-ardships? – Ye dunno,
ye mother's pansy-boys, what hardships is."

Then would ensue some story from his youth,
some yarn of honour tried and courage tested,
such as that tale of boat-drill off the Cape,
pulling the cutter in a house-high sea,
in pains that made him wish he'd not been born,
pains of his backside squirming on the thwarts -
"Seventeen salt-water boils I's on my ass,"
says he, grimacing, "but I dassn't goo sick,
for fear I miss a dollop o' leave I'm doo
when we's back to Pompey agin." We do our best,
given such edifying instances,
to show a manlier bearing on parade.

There was a sadness in Chief Barker's soul,
a trouble glinting in a moistened eye,
a fear that war would end, and his discharge
send him to that bleak country called Outside,
where no one knows or wants to learn a drill,
and no one cares to hear of duty done
in days when ships were ships and men were men.
England could never reasonably expect
more of him, so England would, no doubt,
expect he'd take his leave and fade away.

But there's a spectre comes upon a man
telling him how his usefulness is done
when he retires; and how the world is now
no more the ground in which he grew and grafted.
What stay with him are memories of pains
endured long since, the maculate account
of follies, misadventures, virtues won
out of expediency, hardships endured
wanting alternatives. All flesh is grass,
the twelves roll on, man goeth to his long home –
with seventeen salt-water boils on his ass.

[Glossary: *pusser* Navy, "regular Navy"; *pusser* from "purser", paymaster:
thwarts, cross-benches, pronounced as "thoughts"; *Pompey* = Portsmouth;
the twelves roll on – the enlisted sailor's cry is "roll on my twelve", ie the
period (of years) for which he has enlisted]

BAND MUSIC
(*alla marcia* Tune: "Ubi Sunt")

Where are they now,
euphonium and tuba
in the bands of yesteryear – where are they now? -
trombone
and the cornet´s all-alone
with cymbal´s rattling, trumpet´s prattling, Strauss
or Sousa,
say : where are they now?

"Gone", beats the drum,
gone to the last recording,
to bars of rest in the shining west
and the parks of Kingdom Come.
"Gone, gone, gone",
to meet a Judge awarding
their silver cups to runners-up
their gold shields to some –

Where are they now,
the brainy and the bonny
in the gangs of yesteryear – where are they now,
who laughed,
were sensible or daft,
ambitions reckoning, futures beckoning, brave
and sunny –
tell : where are they now?

"Gone", beats the heart
gone to the past preserving,
to the fall of man on the pension plan,
and the wreck of the apple cart.;
"gone, gone, gone",
deserving, undeserving,
to lie abed with the friendly dead,
or sleep far apart –

Wherever now:
Where they are now:

Forever now.

THE ALMOST-RECOGNITION

Never to pass the end of a certain street
but go the long way round;
to refuse the promptings of scent, the bittersweet
provocations of sound;

to bar from the mind night-thoughts that pry
through fissures of sleep, disallow
the passage of a smuggled memory,
to cry "not now"

when the heart is already inclined to the plea of "then";
all such evasions are vain;
for our hopes are forever on the *qui vive* for when
the past comes again

in a guise of scent or sound or casual sight,
and out of our sadness we bless
the almost-recognition of something that might
have been happiness.

Love and Friendship

.... a time to embrace and a time
to refrain from embracing

Ecclesiastes 3: 5

"I REMEMBER EVERYTHING"

No greater the gap between
the tousled summer beach,
the boy with his pockets full
of shells and elaborate stones
and this old man
blessing the memory,

no farther the long haul
that separates the girl
of sweetest seventeen
(now going on seventy nine)
from this old man
mourning the interval,

but greater, farther, more
than any reach of mind
is his, the inner eye
reviewing everything;
from this old man
nothing escapes unseen,

and so no sense of loss
troubles his waking hours,
no mishap, as in dreams;
only the daily fret
of this old man
mislaying his spectacles

APPARITIONS

The lady on the Jacobean stair,
the monk who sidles through the cloister wall
at twelve o'clock; the rider on the moor
seen by the slanting moon; such ghosts are all
pictorial phantoms, soon identified
as revenants to grace a tourist guide,

less subtle than the sharp remembered scent,
the board that creaks to some forgotten tread
up in the attic; oddly evident
objects back in their places, long mislaid -
these are our common spooks; when we're alone
their tremor startles, like the telephone.

But even these are of a coarser kind,
grosser in substance than the ghosts that dwell
in the synaptic threadings of the mind;
there, spirits leap, but never to the will
of dupe or medium; rise by day or night
in dreamspace, in the sun, in the half-light.

A spectral image of an promise made
in a suburban garden, all these years,
troubles the summer dawn; and here's a shade
mouthing ill-chosen words, miming the tears
shed at a parting; and the wraith, regret,
sad, smiling implacably, stalking me yet.

Memory? conscience? call it what you please,
but feel the ghost, a plaintive haunt that lies
boxed in the brain, not bound to time or place,
like other shades; there's no avoiding these
visions whose poignant visitations lapse
only with death; not even then, perhaps.

For then, perhaps, they wander through time past,
speaking in whispers to some distant grief.
Memorially, ghost reverts to ghost,
in transmutations, bringing back to life
the lady on the stair, whose tears appal
the monk who sidles through the cloister wall.

THE FALL OF MAN

The sin is not the taking of the fruit;
temptation is a branch of innocence.
It is the lies, the lies that follow suit.

Sweet love can do no wrong (but any brute
skilled in deceit can offer that defence).
The sin is not the taking of the fruit.

It is the consequence, the absolute
demise of decency and common sense,
and the whole pack of lies that follow suit.

The broken promises, affairs en route
to new deceits, the maimed intelligence –
the sin is not the taking of the fruit.

It is the hardening within, the mute
refusal to confront the evidence,
and all the sweaty lies that follow suit.

So easily man falls; the grade's acute,
the steps are little, but the drop's immense.
The sin is not the taking of the fruit.
It is the lies, the lies that follow suit.

REMEMBERING DORRIE

That voice of hers could make a stranger duck
at twenty feet, it was a voice
to eviscerate a tradesman and subdue
a taxi driver, a loud, peremptory, British,
refrigerating sort of voice, and it made me laugh,
because her bluebell gaze,
candid, undeceiving, vulnerable, like a child's
who insists on knowing, protested her innocence.

We were once on a crowded train,
in a compartment full of pinstripes and papers,
when she asked, in that voice of hers,
precise as the cut of a crystal, What is nooky?, and
see, the pinstripes immersing in *The Times*, or
botanising in the slideshow fields, and me
muttering ask me later,
but she, bless her, never had time for later.

Later than that were the laters
when I said I loved her, and hoped I was telling the truth,
but I was lying,
and she knew full well I lied, and in that voice of hers,
accusatory, piercing, exacting, pained,
pinned me down to the knowledge of my guilt.
When we parted
her blue eyes sought my face for explanations.

One night she came to me gently in a dream,
and I did not lie – how can one lie to the dead? -
but she knows the truth of me by now, and her voice,
that voice of hers,
the clear, cool voice, was inflected with forgiveness,
and still the blue eyes looked at me with love,
and I woke, happy and weeping for no reason
except the ache of being reconciled.

THE PEARSHAPED SUMMER

Summer went pearshaped, we said;
the bottom fell out of it – too much unavailing,
too much rain on all too many a day,
too many hopes failing;
saddest of all, too many people dead
who played with us once, when we had time to play.

Blame the weather, old age,
bad legs, fatigue, blame God if it comes to that;
something, we said, has pulled our summers awry,
something has fallen flat,
whatever it is, some power we cannot gauge
is at work on the shape of our lives, before we die.

Love, let's deny our plight,
and let's not study again the tears of things,
or look at the doleful face tomorrow wears;
last summer's memory brings
glimpses of gardens and the brief sunlight
and a taste for life, like the cool, sweet tang of pears.

UNDESERVING NATIVE

Missionary zeal, my darling,
ever intolerant
of piled ancestral skulls and tribal rites,
required the savage to wear underpants
and honour the Queen
with all her splendid soldiers
or earn his daily bread at a bully's hand
and sing his way into saintliness.

But what shall we say, my dearest,
of you, saving me
from my archaic masculine habitudes?
("What! Change my shirt? What's wrong with this I've on?")
Bully me as you may
with tender loving care,
no missionary zeal, I hope, will goad me
into respectability.

COMPATIBLES
(for A.J.T,)

At our infrequent meetings we are sure
to resurrect some sentence left alone,
waiting completion, fifteen months before;

then sudden screeds and cackling telephone
report our latest , and each episode
telling the new, invokes the always known,

fraught with a sense of something "understood",
like predicates in Latin, sir, for we
are babes forever in a private wood

speaking the vulgar, quite proficiently
whether as scholar John or messmate Jack,
but always tuned to one insistent key,

which is the song of sixty years turned back
to where a friendship started, once again
rehearsing heydays like an almanac;

and there´s no proposition can explain.
the strength of old affection, or the why,
more than the simple candour of Montaigne:

" it was because he was he and I was I "

FAREWELL TO MY FANCY

(for Katherine Bosley, *doyenne* of churchwardens)

When I was very young,
or even fifty-two,
Katherine, ah Katherine
what might I have been to you?
I would have led you a dance,
you would have taught me the tune,
in the old, old way of a fine romance
in the evermore light of the moon –
but that was then…..

When I was seventeen,
with all my teeth and hair,
Katherine, ah Katherine,
what were you doing, and where?
we could have gone to the "flicks"
and "necked" in the one-and-nines,
and talked about marriage and politics,
and compared our zodiac signs,
but that was then…..

When I was eighty-one,
and hardly able to stand,
Katherine, ah Katherine,
had I been yours to command
when were you mine to obey,
inclined as I am to fall
for the prettiest women, what can I say?
I never *fell down* at all,
but that was then….

This world, I have been told
will end in a fiery surge,
Katherine, ah, Katherine,
then you and I will *merge*
(with Mr Bosley, of course,
to see we do nothing amiss),
at last united in divorce,
Sealed With A Liquefied Kiss;
but until then…….

THE OLD SPAGNOLETTA

Old age has prized into my lung
and wrenched me at the hip –
but should you think, because of that,
I´d lost the will to skip,
come lass, we´ll dance a step or two,
by way of fellowship.

Because my head is full of prayers
and thoughts of right and wrong,
did you suppose, because of those,
I´d lost a lover´s tongue?
I´ll tune the instrument, dear girl,
and treat you to a song.

Because the world has turned away
from times our world has seen,
never be sure that I have done
with all my heart has been;
still you may see the boy in me,
vainglorious, and eighteen.

What of the desert in the throat,
the blizzard in the eyes?
Life being more than flesh can bear,
the flesh lies down and dies;
but love will dance our evening out,
and after sleep, we rise.

LINES FOR MY LASS

1. Noon in the plaza

And such a sweetness in the dancing air,
such a benevolence; the tall sunshine
invites us to enjoy, while we are able,
the shade of noonday sidling through the square.
Come, here´s our café, here´s our usual table,
sit down, and let us take a glass of wine,

and talk together of indifferent things:
of how the nights grow cooler, of how faces
can seem familiar, how former fashions
always come round again; our ageing brings
small, local pleasures – more exalted passions
now dwell in exile in abandoned places.

We lived among them once. There was a cup
of deep delight; we filled it to the brim
and gulped the Spring and heady Summer seasons;
now let us drink our Autumn, sip by sip,
unsay our says and reason with unreasons,
and nose the fragrance at the glass´s rim.

And while we talk distractedly, our eyes
will point the subtle converse of a scene
where implications dance; the glances catching
at something inexpressible and wise.
The muted, nodded pledge, the glasses touching
will sound the depth of all that we have been.

2. *So we were then*

So

long we have known each other
we do not finish our
Sentences, and Verbs
go all uncomplemented
or catch at Objects not
needing to be expressed;
in the childless house of the Subject
no need for any but

We

who sat by the hearthside
at night, and heard the wind
parsing the fretfulness
of the clouded sky, or the rain´s
syllabic muttering
in clauses under the eaves;
our discourse moves among Nouns
showing what happy times

Were

when we were young and able
to turn a brilliant Phrase
or reduce a joy to the clasp
of an orderly Predicate.
Yet no one, dear, who loves you
as much as I do now
would argue that words were truer

Then

3. Otherdays

She moved always
so pertly, with such neat
and nimble feet
and small, swift hands
in the morningland
of otherdays,

danced in her grace,
and with such comeliness;
A kind hostess,
her laughter like a rill
of glittering water, shrill,
silvery; her face

a mirror to the moods
of friends; as I recall
the gleaming fall
of hair, the raven-black
silk at her back,
memory broods

on beauty lost,
its wonderment lopped.
Puritan Time has cropped
that shining elegance.
Now seasons dance
awkwardly into frost,

a grey hour arrives,
limping towards the night;
yet still she is honour-bright
my bonny girl, my lass.
All that she ever was
gleams in her, and survives

4. The question

"How's my boy?" she will say,
in the morning when we stand;
I, shaving brush in hand,
she, bearing tea and toast -
the start of another day,
no different from most.

And I, then, "How's my love?",
while she rummages for her shoes,
and I am instructed to choose
respectable underwear
in case of a sudden move
to a bed in Intensive Care.

We itemise each pain,
assessing its degrees
in arthritic hips or knees
as bearable, at best,
and discuss whether last night's rain
might account for the wheeze in my chest.

We can remember a time
when the day put an end to the night,
and prompt as a flash of delight
the body would sport with the mind
as reason answers to rhyme,
but the heydays are left behind,

and we live, my girl and I,
in dread of a day to come
when lad or lass will be dumb
to question, "How's my own?",
for one may no longer reply,
and one will be left alone.

5. The last need

Now we have need of courage, now the heart
must serve us in this last redoubt of living,
this barrack of old age; come, dearest friend,
who had such art
to school me in the disciplines of loving.
You taught me to begin. Help me to end.

Beauty´s awry and health´s amiss. All flesh
is paper, crumpled by the years, and by them
anxiety is bred, and furtive pain.
Sweet love, refresh
your conquest of these upstarts. Come, defy them.
They will go down and we shall rise again.

They are not of our spirit; the uncouth
burden of sickness, age that slowly, dully,
baffles the hearing, overclouds the sight.
Come, my heart´s youth,
come, my companion in the darkening valley,
and arm in arm let us address the night.

REFLECTIONS

July; the little river feels its way
past a parade of willows, mustering
green and silver along the bank; branches
reach up and hoist the tented sky; flustering
breeze flings out a flag of cloud; to-day
struts jubilant forever down these reaches.

No space now for reflection: rumpled glass
of morning dislocates the trees, and water,
fractured, warps the scene in sudden swirls
of puddled green or spill of sky-blue after
an oarsman tugs the film awry; the gloss
of the fickle mirror melts in sightless whorls.

And no time now to bring to mind again
all that the faithless years have merged, or changed;
memory stirs among the fugitive shapes,
the once-beloved, the dead, the long-estranged;
broken and blurred on a shadow-glass within,
they show by tremulous glimpses, and escape.

But the wind lapses by evening, and calm light,
levelling the glass, placidly reaffirms
strong presences, articulated, whole,
steadfast at length; their valedictory forms
exactly pillared in a silver-bright
analogue of the sky: before nightfall.

Walter and Helen

LOOKING AT THE WAR
A School Prefects Group, 1944.

"Hold it!" the cameraman said, and "still!" and his flash
burst briefly on the assembled ranks, affixing
a choice of expressions. One or two of them smiled,
like sonny at mid-row-front, grinning for England,
and some were patient and satisfied, like winners
who can afford to wait for their successes,
one or two little short of scornful, asking
what on earth is the point of any of this?
They were looking at the war, asking, perhaps,
where they might hope to be just one year on.
So they went away to find out, and it is useless
to ask where they are now, they are always held
In the still memorial posture where they were
one afternoon of mutable English weather
in the spring of the year when Monte Cassino fell

Barrow Grammar School — Summer 1944

Front row: (left to right)
Henry Green   Bill Lewis Mr E S Elwood (Deputy Headmaster) Walter Nash (Head Prefect) Mr S M Price (Headmaster) Gordon Cain Bill Slater
Second row:
Brian Bland   Jack Williams   Bill Gosling   Bill Cain Alan Langtree Cedric Moxon   Kenneth Last
Back row:
Bernard Long Duncan Nixon Eric Phizacklea John Hepple Harry Lister Jack Edmondson

With acknowledgements to *Barrow-in-Furness in the Early 1900's*
Website http://lindal-in-furness.co.uk/history/barrow-industry

This picture shows the waymark of my childhood and youth: the very tall
and extremely powerful "250 ton" crane standing on the quayside at the
Devonshire Dock in Barrow. As a nine-year-old I glimpsed it every day as I
walked to school.

My father worked a lifetime as an engineer at the Yard. In 1948 I worked
some summer months as an unskilled labourer, "mate" to an electrician.

Now in 2009 the Yard is closed, the workers "laid-off", the docks destined
for conversion to a leisure centre and theme park. But the great crane, I
hope, will keep its place as an emblem and memorial of the pride and
power that once were.

Late News

All the labour of man is for his mouth,
and yet his appetite is not fulfilled.

Ecclesiastes 6: 7

i Change and Decay

" change and decay in all around I see"

Henry Francis Lyte, *Abide with me*

MEMORANDA FOR ALL OCCASIONS

Hear what your nose is saying before you go to leave the house.
Did you leave a pan on the stove? Is bread ablaze in the toaster?
Is the garbage out?
Did you flush – oh, you did? Well now, that's all right,

then note what your eyes are explaining as you navigate the street
about the manhole cover and the crossing light and the curb
where the last remains
of doggies'dinners await the unwary foot,

and obey the instructions written for you by your selective ears
in the matter of automobiles, jackhammers, nannies, yobs,
and all the vowels
announcing the death of English as we know it,

and let your palms report to you first at every chance encounter -
you will know by their feel if the person who gladhands you
is a used archbishop
or a pious car salesman, it's all in the touch,

and finally pay attention to your tongue and its various tastes
in comestibles and conversation shared at lunch,
and don't fill your mouth
with yesterday's words, you never know where they've been

in the times between

BEACH RESORT

Tide drops in on the arm of the moon,
the suntan crowd will be following soon,
bold boys showing off abs and pecs
to lustrous girls in tinted specs -
this is a beach resort,
sport;
sea swaggers in and flounces out,
and hasn't a clue what the games are about

Incoming tide has overlaid
sandcastles built with bucket and spade;
now mummy is knitting cable stitch
while daddy pegs out a cricket pitch -
or even a tennis court -
(short);
sea rambles in and walks away,
not raring to know the state of play.

The afternoon's a ball of heat,
shadows revert to the dancers' feet,
prostrate on towels or lounger-beds
makers of markets nod their heads
at rumour and report
(abort);
sea takes a minute and passes on,
noting a closure half begun

Tide's on the turn and ebbing slow,
then faster, as the moon lets go,
old folk huddling in deck chairs
stop reading novels and take to prayers
of a beseeching sort,
(support);
sea hisses and claps as dark descends,
not giving a toss how the story ends.

ONE DEAF POET

Small garden-voices gossiping on their stems,
the chaffinch´s pebble of song, are lost to me.
my ears are closed to intricate device.
Somewhere aloft, the lark is dropping stitches,
but I miss the click of the needles. Music shrinks.
Listening hard, I grasp only the gross
purport of the notes; the delicate
harmonics flutter briefly and elude me.

Audition´s edifice crumbles. Bricks and bats,
wreckages of dry consonants, high vowels,
tumble out of my belfry, and the chimes
ring tinnily for vespers. Grumpy, I lurk
suspiciously in the neighbourhoods of whispers.
"You have to shout," visitors are instructed;
the more they shout the less I am informed..
Shouting is amplifying formlessness.

How common talk distorts to comedy!
"Another slice of bread" reaches me as
"An overflight of dread", and "aftermath"
as "have to bath". I hear a garbled text
by Spooner, muttering in Wonderland:
affable salesmen say, "This marble´s aid
uppers a cistern with your healing pogrom."
Cisterns and marbles will not heal me much.

But what of that? Neighbours, I am a poet,
I am an auditorium to myself.
Hooped in the strict confinement of my skull
elated wings of rhythm lunge and dart;
rustles within shape the sonorities
of forms, measures, sounds in permutations
and patterned mazes, seeking, endless, endless,
a resurrection and the hope of heaven.

Thank heaven, I am not deaf, after all

POEM IN OLD AGE

("Why is a raven like a writing desk?" – the Mad Hatter's unanswered riddle)

They are right, I suppose; age turns you into a child
with defective table manners and a pot belly,
and when even the dustman's assistant calls you Billy
your dignity is impaired; but the more you are riled
the more you are patronised; allowed your quirks
by physicians who query the state of your waterworks,

and surrounded by mourners-in-waiting who cheerfully stand
alert at the drop of a heart to send for the parson,
though meanwhile they talk through your ears in the third person –
"He looks well", "Is that his normal colour?", and -
should your expression suggest you are deaf, or mad,
bend down to bawl in your face and address you as *Dad*.

Just look at the sorry state of you as you slouch
through the evening of life (it's more of a limp than a saunter)
while your whole demeanour suggests the arrival of winter:
the wind blows shrill, the sky bodes ill as you crouch
warming your hands (or your butt) by a fire that dies
into clinkers and ash, the heart and soul of Here Lies.

But must I endure these dismal monitions? No,
suspend the bib, the waterproof bedding, the zimmer,
allow me at least some feeble semblance of summer,
blow me no withering wind, spare me the snow;
I speak, I write, I am; fetch me my slate
and watch the words form: I am articulate,

and if you must set a place on the face of the clock,
no "evening of life", if you please, but late afternoon,
Mad Hatter time, when the talk goes on and on,
and creature fantasies come to riddle and mock,
until I am sweetly inclined to nod off to heaven,
quitting my writing desk (and ignoring the raven).

SO LONG AT THE CLINIC

The worst of it, isn't the waiting bit.
It's your anxiety bears the crucial strain;
to be as ill as this, you have to be fit.

No one complains, no one is going to quit.
Though the expense of time beggars the brain,
the worst of it is not the waiting bit.

Our faces drawn, our eyes switched off, we sit
like travellers on some lost, uncoupled train.
To be as ill as this you must be fit.

Dark non-event is all too brightly lit;
the fear is bad, and in the mind the pain
is worse - and far worse than the waiting bit.

Happy the few who leave with their remit,
under instructions to report again.
To be as ill as this, you try to be fit.

What doctor says may scarify the wit,
whether pronounced in code or spoken plain.
The worst of it is never the waiting bit.

Your life is in your hands - the grief of it
being that your hands have too much to sustain.
The worst of it, isn't the waiting bit.
To be as ill as this you have to be fit.

LOST OBJECTS

Another day that disappears,
another hour of memory destroyed,
one minute more when objects in plain sight
become invisible, and good ideas,
yesterday-bright,
slink off into some dim Platonic void.

Where do they go, the missing words,
the diary, the pocket-watch, the keys?
Here they are, surely, yet they live elsewhere
with wraiths of poems and lawyers´ business cards;
the *facts* are clear,
perception has migrated overseas

to some superior territory
where things are never lost, never mislaid,
and least of all forgotten; where the maps
agree with all the signs, where memory
admits no lapse,
where all elusive details are displayed,

while we are chafed in puzzlement,
irked at the casual absence of our lives,
how they by small departures fret away.
It is the picayune disablement
of day to day
that wounds, and warns, at length nothing survives.

Racked and speechless in last hours,
when no word fits and nothing makes a.match
we quit the premises, and leave behind
nothing that matters: our inheritors
are left to find
the house-keys, the bad poems, the pocket-watch

ii   *Getting and losing*

The world is too much with us; late and soon
Getting and spending, we lay waste our powers

William Wordsworth, *Miscellaneous Sonnets xxxiii*

INSTANT ACCESS

There was a moorland height my boyhood knew,
a scrambled climb in places, where we went
on hands and knees;
                when by degrees
we´d got the better of the gruff ascent
a burnished ocean let us praise the view.

It´s different nowadays. The old hilltop,
girdled with access roads, is conquered fast;
paths, trimly kept
                guide the inept,
the multivarious cars go bawling past,
the view is free to all who care to stop.

Wonderment bleaches; we have come too far.
All things unreachable are given to us,
in films we plumb the seas,
                quiz the Hesperides,
alighting from the air-conditioned bus
stride over mountains in a cable car.

Progress, insistent, worries into being
the once exempt; ardours are possible
any week day -
                see, on display
a world made instant and accessible.

If therefore barely worth a second seeing.

MAKEOVER

Today´s vogue is for Makeover –
reconstitution of your domestic schemes
when your bed and your bath and your gloryhole under the stairs
are ripped out, ruthlessly, by expert teams
who then take over
totally, and build you the homes of your wildest dreams,
which are real nightmares.

Myself, I prefer Shoveunder
for tidying-up. I do not like your sleek
patternless fabrics, clean lines, intrusions of brick,
or your plaster pillars modelled on the Greek,
and I wonder
when the clients open their eyes for that little peek
they are not instantly sick.

What do they feel, Dayafter,
when the drawn curtains make bereavement plain?
Where is the cordial mess, the clutter, the orphaned shoes,
the sagging bookshelf, the historic stain,
the old laughter,
all made over à la mode, and how can you choose
to make it again?

They should call it Fakeover,
it is like moving house for moving´s sake –
that kind of motion´s a foolish move, too soon, too far,
on the wrong premises; a gross mistake,
don´t make it, rover,
wear slippers, and whatever steps you take
stay where you are..

THINGSHIP

King Thing, head of a line
not always on display
but never discontinued,
distinguished scion of
the House of Azda-Tesco
serves all his people

with special offers at
prices they can afford.
On state occasions
Archbishop Visa and
the earl of Barclaycard
make the arrangements, and

"Live forever!" the ranks
of High Street banks proclaim,
and "Thing, forever live!"
comes the financier's call,
whose fealty secures
our State of Thingship, while

choirs of shelfstackers sing
in St.Safeways Cathedral,
anthems our fathers loved,
praising the Thing of Things:
"Buy two and get one free",
or "While stocks last".

WE PIN-BALL MACHINES

We are almost human, we pin-ball machines.
See how for money we consent to click
To chatter to wink to glitter to jerk to giggle
almost humanly; lusting
with stertorous with shuddering concupiscent haste
after the belly-dancer, after the speedway rider,
after the cowboy's candid teeth and leather loin.
After the gangster's gun.
After the dragon-hoarded pile of gold.

Almost humanly we trust in Chance, though
come night in our Arcade, conviction dies.
Mammiferous Lady Luck is pallid, the hopalong lariat
whirls aimlessly among the shambling cattle; wheels
roar lustreless, gunblaze cools, gold mimics lead,
colour is leached away, as logic fades
from human dreams.
Darkly through languid glass
loiter the symbols daytime agitates.

Then click-jerk-quick-as-a-wink we are up and about,
snapping at each other, bickering, nattering
in the random non-stop-slap-and-tickle disjointed
directionless quicksilver code
of the almost humanly improvident;
cacchinating from hope to hope, nagging
this oracle or that, perversely
simulating joy with stuttering baubles; waiting
for lover or victim to come to make us decide to
succeed .

PHANTOMS OF THE OPERA
(Mozart / da Ponte, *The Marriage of Figaro*)

Dear *Count*, your imagination
of yourself as death to women,
- jealous as hell if thwarted -
is something we all enjoy,
though even the dimmest spectator
perceives in the strut of suspicion,
behind the satin and bluster,
the wraith of a clumsy boy.

And epicene *Cherubino*,
warbling to shame the angels,
your notion of love´s a romantic
white horse you will never mount,
but when your voice is broken
and you´re back from your hitch in the army,
with the spoils of war in your trousers,
you ´ll greatly resemble the Count.

The manly man among you
is *Figaro*, without question,
with a lucky knack of survival
by playing the game and the rules,
but even he, in the darkness
when a tremor of doubt assails him
can only moan about women
and damn all men as fools.

He´s lost without *Susanna*,
who´s never lost for an answer,
a plucky girl and witty,,
loyal to lover and friend,
maidservant to a *Countess*
wronged by a lump of a husband,
who duly gets his come-uppance,
and a pardon, at the end.

It gleams on us in the shimmer
of a theatre´s painted action,
that pardon, for our presumption,
our impotent sorrow and rage;
the grace of Amadeus
absolves us, in our darkness,
from the fret of those busy phantoms
we mock on the brilliant stage.

BELOW THE STOCKBROKER BELT

Where once the Saxon pegged his thatch
and scoured the copse to feed his fire
our dwellings stand, secure, aloof,
each tented roof
the emblem of a heart's desire.

Peaceful: less than one hour from town,
extensive views, commodious grounds;
wistaria round the cottage walls
demurely falls.
(Freehold: £900,000)

The blackbird in the flowering bush,
the Bentley nestling in the drive -
such simple things in England now
inform us how
content we are to be alive.

Each labours for his just reward,
but in the scale of righteousness
anything under 90K,
though in its way
commendable, is poor success.

Life is unjust to some, perhaps,
sinners rise up and saints fall flat;
but in our world of which-is-which
the good are rich,
the bad are poor. Amen to that.

SELBY

We called him Selby, not
after a coalfield up in Yorkshire, though
God knows, he was a grimy beggar, but
because, poor chap, he was so plainly past
his sell-by date. Our little joke, you know:
our guess that his next meal could be his last.

He took his food in pain
being almost toothless, could not chew his meat,
but bolted it in gobs; he was unclean,
dirt-scarred, from fights, or sleeping rough, perhaps;
decency had abandoned him; a sheet
of thickened spittle hung around his chops.

In sunny Tenerife
wild cats like Selby are a common sight,
where children in sweet innocence receive
the Christmas gifts that summer throws away;
the furry toy they cuddled on Twelfth Night
put out to pine in hell come Easter Day,

to forage, fight or fall,
to fornicate with strangers, to beget
unsightly brats, to live life to the full –
much like a human, on uncertain terms -
until he´s caught and neutered by the vet
or done to death by violence or his worms.

Well, as for Selby, we
felt that his sufferings had gone too far.
It would be kind, we said, to set him free,
to have him put to sleep; it would be kind
to catch him by the river, as it were,
and ferry him to lasting peace of mind.

But what a fight he made!
You might have thought that he would understand,
somehow, the benefits of being dead.
Is the sunlight so dear? You might have thought
a lick of cream, a browse at garden's end,
hardly worth fighting for. But still he fought.

Then went to be put down,
abstracted to the past, a scheme devised
more for our civil comfort than his own.
So with all things beyond their sell-by date;
so with all lives outcast, outworn,.despised,
by the Lord given; stifled by the State

iii   Political animals

"man is a political animal"

Aristotle

PORTRAIT OF A STATESMAN

".....paint my picture truly like me...remark
all these roughnesses, pimples, warts,
 and everything as you see me....."
Oliver Cromwell, to his portrait painter, Peter Lely.

He said, "Look – you know –
I don´t pretend – I mean, I think
I´m a pretty straightforward
sort of chap – you know – I
like to be upfront
whenever I can, that´s not to say
as far – you know – and – I mean –
more than ready to talk to the press,
man to man – or womanofcourse – and
to the public just let me say,
what you see is what you get."

So to the waiting scribes
with singular eloquence
in the style of a simple man
appealing to his peers
he drew his discourse out
spinning a pleasant web
of almost rational
might-be argument.
Candour so well expressed
gave an illusion of grace,
but the gaps in his character showed
like the warts on Cromwell´s face.

SPEAKING OF HEROD

Someone should put in a decent word for Herod.
Say what you will, you know where you stand with him.
He's not all PR boloney, showmanshite,
like the clowns who come to rallies and conferences,
with their speeches rigged and their faces artfully tanned -
slapping the pancake on and showing their teeth -
to be a sight to frighten the turnstiles
and to be the boring of the people - Israel
has had better kings than Herod, and may have worse,
but this you would have to say, he gets things done.
He keeps a police presence - what's wrong with that?
He keeps well in with Rome - what's wrong with that?
He doesn't shrink from having to do the ungraceful -
you whinge about a couple of dozen first-born,
but what were they doing, getting first-born in the first place?
Two sides to it - you'll say "dictatorship",
I 'd say, no, "the slap of firm government"
(and hey, when he slaps, he slaps, I grant you that)
But ask yourself, if this world of ours is a tent,
isn't it better to have him peering out,
with us, than have him riled, and peering in?
He's a good old boy. We should be proud of him.
I 'd be ready to say, the man's an *idealist*.
History, you bet, will see him justified.

THEM BATRACHIANS

Joe says, "I'm not a racist, personally,
not me, not personally, no, I'm not.
I'm easy with them Batrachians, as a rule –
they've one down at the club, tending the bar.
Many's the personal chat I've had with him.
I call him "Froggy eyes", and *he* don't mind,
being the sort can take a joke. Some can't.
I wouldn't fuss if they was all like him.
It's just – there are so so many of 'em, see?
You tell me why it is, they're *everywhere,*
flooding this country, taking houses, jobs –
Get yourself down the market, Saturday,
it's chock-a-block with them Batrachians. Straight.
It ain't their being green, or that, it ain't
the eyes, it ain't the way their tongue shoots out,
it ain't the stuff they eat (which turns my guts).
Live and let live is what I say – it's just,
let's face it, they ain't *British.* Are they now?"
So says Joe; and I, coward, drink my tea.

ELECTIONS

Things were otherwise
in distant times when leaders chose themselves
with muscle and magic and an evil eye.
Choice didn't take too long,
no longer than it might to drop a rock
or push a rival into a lion's mouth
and there you were,
undoubtedly the one man for the job

Even when kingdoms came
brute force was not completely out, but then
being the Lord's anointed helped a lot.
You could feel pretty safe
with oil on your head and Latin in your mouth,
and psalmodies of bishops to acclaim
divine inheritance;
when *they* acclaimed you, you just *stayed* acclaimed –

unless you were deposed –
but in the Enlightenment a new day dawned
governance then was more of a gentlemen's club
with classical quotes;
the name of the game was liberty (within reason),
the elected being those who reasoned well
and were at liberty
to hustle for patronage, or buy a vote.

Quite different now, of course,
no bribery for us; our candidates
face trial by vilification, then emerge
all squeaky-clean
in staybrite suits, to explain themselves to the Press
week after week in the name of all that's truly;
it's a protracted test,
but in the end somebody has to lose.

THE OLD ALUMINIUM FACES

Never before has so much been done
For you – for us – for them – well, *everyone*;
Three times as much has been spent on hospitals,
On day-care centres, meals on wheels –
And the poor, who will always have it rough,
Are at least *that little bit* better off,
And can ask for *special help* in *particular* cases
      When our policies take effect,
      Say the old aluminium faces.

Five times as much has gone into building schools
To be sure our children´s children don´t turn out fools
And nearly ten times the sum will be invested
In schemes for having the bright ones tested;
And even the thick, who will always be around,
Will be taught in a way that´s fundamentally sound,
Though you mustn´t expect to see them win any races
      Till our policies take effect,
      Say the old aluminium faces.

If Jesus were here, he´d consider himself *in clover*,
He`d own his own home, he´d be driving a new Range Rover,
He´d see how the taxpayer´s money is spent
To help the righteous to afford the rent;
Of course, you´ve your blacks, and your unemployed, and your old,
And those people who kip in cardboard, out in the cold,
But we´ll slot them all very nicely into their places
      When our policies take effect
      Say the old aluminium faces.

TURNABOUT.
(after *The Old and Young Courtier*, 17thC., Anon.)

From a man of his word and a gentleman bred,
with an Oxford voice and a Roman head,
and a Crown Derby chamberpot under the bed,
 like a Fogey of old,
 a quondam Fogey,

with an elegant ladyship, frosty and lank,
a runagate daughter who's broken the bank,
and a playboy son who's thick as a plank,
 like a Fogey of old,
 a family Fogey,

with pin-striped trousers, a Homburg hat,
a misquotation trotted out pat,
and a smirk on his phiz like the Cheshire cat,
 like a Fogey of old,
 a has-been Fogey,

with ritual manners and hangman views,
with well-rehearsed phrases to put in the news,
and a jailer's view of the freedom to choose ---
 from that old Fogeyman,
 once on a Fogey,

to a rascal who's risen with barely a trace,
with an off-white twang and a butterscotch face,
and an inbuilt instinct for holding his place,
 like the Faker we know,
 new smiling Faker,

a man of the people on company boards,
with a eye for whatever the market affords
and a bottom for warming his seat in the Lords,
 that's Faker made new,
 renewable Faker,

with a talent for lies and arithmetic,
a ready-made hand for the three-card trick,
and a caring heart that bleeds like a brick,
 in the new Faker way
 of the takeaway Faker,

with a wife or a mistress, as he´s inclined,
and a Savile row suit with a big vent behind
for airing his views when he's speaking his mind,
  like the thinker we know,
  fresh-thinking Faker,

with an eye like a fish and a neb like a tyke
and a mouth like a hole in a derelict dyke
spouting statistics, hot air and the like -
  but tell me, who's who,
  Old Fogey, New Faker?

CAESAR IS COMING
(AD 9 and after)

Caesar is coming, there´s never a doubt of it;
hark to the rumour, the rumble, the shout of it;
eagles are winging,
the legions are bringing
freedom for all, and we can´t get out of it.

Rome is the country where matters are settled,
the temples are marble, the highways are metalled,
and not being Romans
makes all other humans
just so many fish to be caught and kettled.

Give up, Arminius, while there´s a chance for you,
gods and the stars may be doing their dance for you,
yet, you poor Herman,
you´re only a German,
and Caesar will spare but a passing glance for you.

Cede: the imperial power will be kind to us,
colonels and magistrates bring peace of mind to us,
sparing the poor,
marching before,
showing a massively proud behind to us.

Soon comes the day when every nation
will flock to render a standing ovation
from grateful hearts
and other parts
to Caesar, passing the frontier station.

Time only will tell the turning about of it,
wisdom resolve the in and the out of it,
who pays the bill
for good or for ill,
but Caesar is coming, there´s never a doubt of it.

A SENSE OF COMPROMISE
(showing at a cinema near you)

The sheriff, gunslung, hero-hipped,
enters the bellowing saloon,
which hushes hollow as a crypt.
The rantipole piano-tune
polkas a bar, then dies away.
Our man, with bandy elegance,
adopts a tailored, killing stance,
and bids the villain make his play.

His leathership is playing cards.
He levers backward in his chair,
stacks up the silence, and discards
two aces and a regal pair;
uncoils himself, his hands poised high,
into a blackness six feet tall.
The place is suddenly too small,
one of the giants has to die.

Toadies and henchmen shuffle clear,
the dove-grey crooked banker glides
into the shadow at the rear,
the broads retire, the barman hides,
while low-cut madam from her door
aloft, looks down without regret.
For good or ill the scene is set:
the lean half-brothers take the floor.

Foregone conclusion! Mister Right
(who shaves and uses brilliantine)
was starred (by God) to win this fight.
Plugging the badman plumb between
the brackets of his beastlyfrown,
he bids the Folks, in baptist voice,
to hear the message, make their choice -
Crime or the Law to rule this town.

Amen, the music says. We stand,
meek, with a sense of *missa est*,
shrugging our coats on, while a grand
plum-coloured blessing paints the West.
Into a neon afterglow
we ride our corporation bus;
the ranch is saved, but not for us,
we just dropped in to see the show.

And glad to see It All Came Out,
go home to supper and the lies
we live when sheriffs aren´t about.
Home to a sense of compromise,
which asks that we maintain the law,
while in our dreams, without reproach,
we screw the women, rob the coach,
and beat young blue-eye to the draw.

iv   ***Night Thoughts***

Twilight and evening bell.
And after that, the dark!

Alfred Tennyson   *Crossing the Bar*

EARLY EVENING TV

Betty the Weathermaid visits in the evening,
a shapely lass with a busy pair of hands,
sweeping the arrows of wind in their fugitive circuits,
round and round, hither and yon
wringing out rain and puffing up cushions of cloud
and talk, talk, talk, talk,
adjusting the belts of high pressure,
talk talk talk talk
planning the week ahead from Monday to Friday
incomprehensibly in phrases
culled from the Weathermaid's thesaurus,
anticyclonically weaving,

till Stan the Anchorman comes with his beefy tale
of war in the middle east, and the stockmarket
on its antepenultimate legs, the price of oil,
the vagaries of the pound against the dollar
talk, talk, talk, talk
of the politician's hotly denied back-hander,
the baby found adrift in the supermarket,
the film star's battle against narcolepsy.
And last the story
of the footballer bought for a cool two million bucks
and the state of his broken toe.

Talk, talk, talk, talk,
Talk talk talk talk
Talktalktalktalk.

Switch off.

ALL HALLOWS

Be at your best tonight, be still and seemly.
Your visitors are walking in the dark,
through a long underpass, a boundless park,
the saints are coming, they are simple, very
benign and ordinary,
their clothes are maculate, their faces homely.

Sit at your meal now, never quit the table
to get the door or lift the telephone,
the saints are coming, your address is known,
much as your heart is known, the ghosts will find you,
they will remind you
of all your sins, as only they are able.

Sit silent at your meal; in solemn token,
break your choice bread and drink your vintage wine
The saints sit mouthless by, and make no sign,
except to spill the tremor from a glass
or, where faint shadows cross,
say something gently – but with no word spoken,

as though familiar voices had reproved you,
inaudibly, you being of their kind
when they were flesh, this evening in your mind
whispering fretfully.of times long gone
with you, their son,
when they advised you, and reproached, and loved you.

COLD STARLIGHT

Proudly tonight the stars present
an act from their tall circus-tent;
we view, from earth below,
bully Orion versus Bear,
while Cassiopeia in her chair
watches the show.

So charmed from childhood, we conspire
to see these figments picked in fire
as old familiar friends,
but Science makes the adult case,
reading the program as a race
to bitter ends.

Flung in the long outreach of night,
untrained, unplanned, a violent flight
of ashes, rubble, rocks,
the ruthless universe expands,
nor means, nor feels, nor understands -
this is what shocks -

to see that starry pantomime,
once testament of the sublime,
the beautiful, the true,
warped in a tract of the absurd.
In the beginning was the Word,
but then it blew.

Scattering coals to catch our eyes,
it leaves the light that laves the sky´s
uttermost seaborne rim
too cold to cheer the simple heart,
but what is man, Lord, that Thou art
mindful of him?

Though all the night-skies´ loveliness
excites the tongue to praise and bless
whatever Time endures,
our thoughts are not the stars´ affair:
as for our comfort, or despair -
no: come indoors.

CANCELLED ADDRESSES

Penstrokes like drivelling sleet
or slant of rain
on a deserted street
deface a page where I shall never again
look for old friends.
Here the news ends

of colleagues, families, wives,
things children say,
our resurrected lives,
wishes and Christmastime and Easter Day;
now rainstrokes form
an arrow-storm.

Striking into the crowd
it thins the ranks
of some who made me proud,
or made me laugh, or gave me cause for thanks;
on each and all
slant showers fall.

I draw a small Christ-cross,
inscribe a date
to calendar the loss
of quiet men and women, who of late
had an address
in liveliness,

and wonder in whose book
my past resides
and who may turn to look
for that blind alley where my name abides
the winter night,
the arrows'flight.

EMBARCATION

Flags of all nations
celebrating the night wind, and the lights
jewelling the port, and passengers
boarding to music, and the quays
gathering to farewell
as the sea glitters a welcome, and the sky
discloses the dark contour of the land.

Ritual occasions
when the vessel sidles grandly from the shore
with the merest relinquishing touch
of regret for auld lang syne
while formalities recede
and resolute the ship takes to the night.
This is the shape departure wishes to be.

Then why these visions
of the parting moment missed, the light switched off,
the traveller in his cabin
shrouded in sudden sleep;
so many goodbyes unsaid
as the ship sails blind, steering no certain course
in the grey and forever race of a pointless tide?

WHAT COMES NEXT

"Comes to all of us", the saying goes
for all of us, sooner or later;
momentum slows,
the future fails, however astute the plan,
the relentless kalends and the takeaway man
corner us, sooner or later.

Memory plays its game with faces and scenes
forever coming and going;
on silent screens
the actors jerk their arms and mime their speech
and shed their tears, and we have tears for each
condemned to coming and going.

Comes to all of us that we are shades,
only awake for sleeping;
old daylight fades
and soon there is none to remember yesterday's face.
Remember me, dear souls, if I get to the place
where we all awake from sleeping.

Epilogue

But if a man live many years and rejoice in
them all; yet let him remember the days of
darkness; for they shall be many.

Ecclesiastes 11: 8

ON THE GO

Keep taking the pills, folks,
stay on the go,
keep taking the pills.

Whatever the state
of your lungs, your liver, your spleen,
your heart, your bladder, your arterial tension.
your eyes, your nerves, your diverticulitis
or arthritis,

Keep taking the pills folks,
however you go,
keep taking the pills

Whatever the tale
of your kith and kissing kin,
your spouse, your mother, your brother, his kids,
your uncle, your cousins removed, stepsister Annie,
or vehement granny,

Keep taking the pills, folks,
go with the flow,
keep taking the pills.

Whatever the case
of the world around you, the wars,
the famines, the new diseases, the floods,
the terrors, the talks about talks, the embassies, missions,
and living conditions,

Keep taking the pills, folks,
let it all go,
keep taking the pills,

Whatever the need
take Credo and Paternoster,
a dose of the Gloria,
Kyrie and Christe eleison
for any occasion,

Keep taking the pills, folks,
be ready to go,
keep taking the pills.

NOCTURNAL

Let a last word in stillness be heard
and nothing louder than whispers
affront the quietude of nesting birds
in their shadowy vespers,

for the heart grows tired of its punctual beat,
and the choral soul refrains
from harmony, and the doors will be shut in the street
and all that remains

will be the recollection of airs that belong
to measures from long ago
in another place, and all the daughters of song
will be brought low.

POSTSCRIPT FROM THE HESPERIDES
(December 2004)

Mañana dawdles in late afternoon;
sundown lolls on his deck above the sea
moon's ghost attends the rising of the moon -
in the Hesperides we pass our time
laboriously not doing overmuch;.
The sky works round the clock; repeatedly
palm and hibiscus stage their pantomime.
Europe is far off; yet we stay in touch.

We've papers here, galore – your *Allgemein*
your *Corriere, Telegraaf, Païs,*
Mundo or *Monde* or *Dagblad*, here's a fine
and fulsome gift of European tongues
babbling away – but then, should language fail,
still we have choice, for here in Paradise,
for the convenience of the package throngs,
they stock the *Mirror* and the *Daily Mail*

So Britain's none too far – yet far enough,
to judge from what the papers say. It.seems
the country is abed, and sleeping rough,
a nightmare slumber in a third-rate hell,
crimes by the streetful, swindles by the load,
lies by the score, in triplicate, in reams,
the likely future a condemned hotel
slumped at the dead end of a potholed road

The Papermen pay court to the Celebs -
privileged helots at a shameless feast,
or else, the honoured tribunes of the plebs,
who represent the people's interest
in football, fashion, and the music scene,
with narcophagic interludes, increased
devotion to pornography, and zest
for fake religions. And God help the Queen

God help us all, indeed, if what they say
is even half-way true - a broad account
up to a point, and in a general way
honestly meant, and almost accurate? –
but look, there's nothing true under the Sun.
"If England were what England seems", I'd count
myself well out of it, expatriate
in body, soul as hotly on the run

But she is not, nor can she be, because
the *patria* is seldom in the press.
The *is* of her is buried in the *was,*
dispersed among remembered moments, caught
out of the dark of lost experience,
split seconds of a lifetime's Englishness,
particles of diverse cognition, wrought
into a pattern of enduring sense.

You watch the points of light that stress the dark,
the separated stars, that meet your stare
as linked and lively constellations - mark,
that's a pure fiction; it is the eye,
reading the night, designs the wheeling crew
of heroes, horses, heroines, bull and bear.
all the palaver of the glittering sky
turned to a narrative your childhood knew.

So with the shapes of *patria*; she exists
in constellations of those hidden stars
figuring in the mind's eye, and persists
through all the stir of reminiscent years
until the starpoints pattern out a whole,
till these perceptions are as avatars
of warnings, prophecies, elations, fears,
the narratives of the wayfaring soul,

in recollections of discrete events,
of words that take heroic meaning in
the context of remembered sounds and scents:
the decent act; assurances that grow
out of the testimony of mute lives;
abiding friendship – there all stars begin.
Such lights I take for warrant, that although
England be lost, the *patria* survives.

See, night comes on. The sun abruptly falls
to the grayblue Atlantic; presently
the tide, wind-flustered, mutters under walls,
columns, riven curtains, of great rocks
towering a thousand feet above the foam.
Darkness enveils the dark; the exile sea,
fretful under these mountains, also knocks
against the headlands of a place called home.

ANNOTATIONS and COMMENTS

Poems should be able to survive and fend for themselves without benefit of commentary, I would generally agree; and there are more than a few poems in this book that need no authorial supervision and perhaps are no longer any of the author's business. But the poems in general are of quite a personal kind, and draw on information randomly lodged in my octogenarian memory, miscellaneous data to which I can hardly expect present readers to have spontaneous and unhindered access. This is particularly true of the poems in the first quarter or third of the book. They speak of persons once famous, of events and ideas once familiar, of bygone household facts and objects. I have thought it necessary to identify not only the who? and the what? but also the when?, giving to some forgotten persons and lost phenomena their memorial position in time.

With this aim in view I provide, here and there, dates — of a life-span, of an event, of a publication or a play, of anything that might slip the mind. The burden of annotation grows lighter for the second half of the book, where fairly recent facts, figures and happenings, require, on the whole, less exposition.

In my comments I draw occasional attention to features of verse-form, though this is perhaps as much to please myself as anyone else.

Early Days

p. 11 **Beforehand** In this poem throughout, penultimate syllables "chime" with line-final words eg. "anger"/ "sang"/ "atlas"/ "that".

Lines 2-3 "Rudyard Kipling....... in every patch and parish of the atlas " refers indirectly to Kipling's poem *Recessional*:

> God of our fathers, known of old
> Lord of the far flung battle-line,
> Beneath whose awful Hand we hold
> Dominion over palm and pine."

This was written for Queen Victoria's Diamond Jubilee (1897), two years before the Boer War (1899-1901), the object of much "imperial anger".

Line 22 "gods": the uppermost gallery in the theatre, with the cheapest seats; location of a vociferous, hypercritical audience.

Line 27 "Dear Land of Hope and Glory" refers to the Coronation anthem for Edward VII, written by A C Benson (1862-1925), and set to the trio section of Elgar's Pomp and Circumstance March Nr. 1 Opus 39.

p 12 *An Old Photograph*

Line 7 "Pals" you are called": "Pals" were volunteers for service in the "new army" being raised by Lord Kitchener in 1915--16. A "pals" batallion was a unit composed of volunteers from the same region, the same town, the same block of streets, as in this photograph. they trained together, went to France together, and mostly died together, or were dispersed to other units. The photograph labelled by the photographer "Barrow-in-Furness Pals 1915" was one my mother often showed and spoke about; of the two men who "came home", one was her brother (my uncle Tom). The other was "invalided out", broken in mind.

Line 27 "Loos", the Battle of Loos, September--October 1915, at which the British lost some 70,000 men. "Somme", the Battle of the Somme, July--November 1916, a struggle in which the Allies (British and French) lost 600,000 men to gain a few kilometres of ground.

p. 13 *With Puns and Paper Aeroplanes*

Line 6. "Joe Grimaldi", Joseph Grimaldi (1778-1837). "Joey", legendary prince of clowns, supreme in music hall and pantomime, and famed for his "routines", whether vocal or visual — the latter a kind of dumbshow, using as supporting props diverse objects lying to hand on stage. I am told that professional clowns still talk of "doing a Joey", with reference to improvisations of that kind.

Lines 20--21. *Ombra mai fú,* an aria in Handel's opera (Serses "Xerxes"), this being the tune popularly known as "Handel's *Largo: Traumerei* ("Day-dreaming") piano piece in Schumann's Kinderscenen (Scenes from Childhood).

p 16 *A Line Held*

Line 4. "gas mantle"; a gauze cover fitted over the gas jet to make an incandescent light.

Line 13. "cuts"; Strictly, pictures, illustrations (the earliest "cuts" in journalism were actually prints from wood cuts); however, the word may denote, more generally, "items of interest".

Line 17. "snap"; the workman's mid-shift snack. My mother's word for this was "tommy", which, I think, was an abbreviation of "soft tommy", meaning "bread". See Eric Partridge's *Dictionary of the Underworld* London 1950.

p. 17 *Northern Washday*

A glossary of implements may be necessary. eg. *copper*, a copper basin, like a round bath, which could be heated from beneath; *dolly legs*, a wooden tripod, set on a long shaft, with a crossbar handle at the top end: used for turning and circulating the clothes in the copper; *posser*, a copper bell, vented, set on a long shaft, used for "plunging" the clothes in the water. cp. French *pousser* to push. The *mangle*, a heavy cast-iron affair with two large rollers, was used for "wringing out" everything from smalls to double bedsheets.

p. 19 *Grandparents*

Line 7 "(the) Pink 'Un" A journal for followers of the horse racing fancy, so called for the colour of the paper on which it was printed.

p. 20 *Little Miss Murray.*   That was her name and her station, and so she was always styled. thus her image, wholly candid, dwells in my memory.

Line 8 "Winegums and lemon drops": sweets chewy or suckable, which she brought to keep us quiet and attentive while she spoke. The lines that separately conclude the four verses are the first four lines of the hymn "Praise, my soul, the King of Heaven" by Henry Francis Lyte (1793--1847)

In line 22, friend is ambivalent, referring apparently to the heavenly friend of line 11, but slantwise to the earthly Miss Murray.

p. 21 *Val Cumberbatch*. In Rugby League Football, a great, indeed legendary, wing three-quarter, famous for his accelerations and changes of step in "running through" opponents. The poem's alliterations and internal rhymes intentionally simulate his attacking "jinking" style. His greatest performance was in an international match against France in Halifax, in 1938, but that is not the match remembered in this poem. My memory of a man gracefully showing what skill means, is of an ordinary "Saturday game", played at Barrow , in the old Northern League, ca. 1937.

p. 22 *London Midland and Scottish* abbr. L M S. Until 1948 (when the railways were "nationalised" as British Rail), a company operating from London (Euston), into the Midlands, Lancashire, Cumberland and points North and West. Its counterpoise was the London and North Eastern, the L N E R, out of St Pancras and Kings Cross to points North and East. In my boyhood fancy, these were the superlanes of Britain.

Line 4 "magical messages": Stephens Ink, Vimto etc. These were advertisements painted on tinplate sheets prominently fixed to station walls or buildings.

Line 13 "Jarrowmen": one of the "hunger marches" of the 1930's in 1936 a protest against unemployment in Jarrow, then running to 80% of the workforce in that town.

Line 31 "that morning in early September" : September 3rd 1939

Line 32 "as the clock struck eleven": at eleven a.m., two hours after sending Hitler an ultimatum demanding Germany's withdrawal from Poland,

Neville Chamberlain, speaking from the Commons, formerly declared war.

Line 35 "sirens": shortly after Chamberlain's broadcast declaring war, a warning siren was sounded in London, giving (false) notice of an enemy approach to the south coast. The sound of its undulating wail soon became familiar as an air-raid warning, together with the steady note that announced the "all clear".

p. 23 *The Conscript*

Line 9 "those camps" ie. the concentration camps in Germany and Poland, about which relatively little was known until after the war in Europe had ended.

Line 14 "tries to rhyme but cannot explain". But it does rhyme— study final and penultimate syllables, eg. "war" — boring", "hell" — "shelter" etc. cp. the "chime scheme" of Beforehand p. 11

p. 24 *Hard Ships*

Epigraph: *et te sonantem* etc.   "and you, Alchaeus, with your golden plectrum, giving full voice to the hardships of a seaman's life."

Glossary: *pusser* Navy: "regular Navy" pusser from "purser", paymaster. *thwarts*, crossbenches, pronounced as "thoughts"; *Pompey* = Portsmouth.

the twelves roll on — the enlisted sailor's cry is "roll on my twelve" ie. the period (of years) for which he had enlisted.

Line 7 "Jutland": the only major sea battle of World War I, fought on 31st May 1916 between two squadrons of battle cruisers, both with heavy losses, each claiming victory.

Line 45 "all flesh is grass" Isaiah 40:6

Line 46 "man goeth to his long home" Ecclesiastes 12:5

Lines 20 and 47. "salt water boils": but these *furuncles* are a dermatitis associated with fishermen (deep-sea) who get them on their arms. Chief Barker (not his real name) was quite positive that his occurred elsewhere, in consequence of squirming on the thwarts.

p. 26 **Band Music**. Subtitle *"Ubi sunt"*: short for *Ubi sunt qui ante nos fuerunt?* — "Where are they now who lived before us?", a trope from mediaeval literature, still alive and working well. Its first occurrence is traceable to Anicius Manlius Severinus Boethius (ca. 480--525) in his *De Consolatione Philosophiae*, Bk II, *metrum* 7 "Ubi nunc fidelis ossa Fabricii manent", Where are they now, the bones of Fabricii the faithful ?

Lines 6-7 "Strauss/ or Sousa". Johann Strauss (1825-1899) the "Waltz King" who also wrote marches (eg. the popular Radetsky March); and John Philip Sousa (1854--1932), the "March King", who wrote, for example, "The Stars and Stripes Forever" and "The Liberty Bell" (the latter now popularly known as the music accompanying the "credits" scroll of the TV programme "Monty Python's Flying Circus")

Love and Friendship

p. 31 *Apparitions*

Line 15 "synaptic threadings of the mind": neural connections —a *synapse* is the point of transfer between adjacent neurons. I should have written "brain" rather than "mind", but was committed to the rhyme from the first line of the stanza.

p. 32 **The Fall of Man** In form this is a *villanelle*: nineteen lines, two rhymes throughout, with alternating refrain-lines, in five tercets, repeated together in a closing quatrain.

p. 35 *Undeserving Native*

lines 2--3. "intolerant of piled ancestral skulls and tribal rites". These lines came to me in recollection of an episode recorded by Sir Arthur Grimble (1885--1956) in his *A Pattern of Islands* (publ. John Murray 1952). Grimble, a civil servant trained in the Colonial Office, became in 1926 Resident and Commissioner in the Gilbert and Ellis Islands Colony. The episode in question was an American evangelist's zealous destruction of the islanders' ancestral shrines. The islanders, Christians, or at least respectful of Christian belief, were deeply wounded by what they regarded as an act of senseless and impious vandalism.

p. 36 **Compatibles** The form is *terza rima*, tercets progressively linked by rhyme **aba, bcb, cdc** etc. until the close which must be **xyz... y...** .   AJT is A J Trott, sometime Head of the English Department at King Edward's School, Birmingham. He and I were at college together, and were inducted into lower-deck life in the Navy at the same time, in 1944: whence "scholar John and messmate Jack". The poem's last line quotes Michel Montaigne (1533-1592) from his *Essais* Vol I nr. xxxviii : *parceque c'était lui, parceque c'était moi* —this in explanation of his love for a dear friend, Etienne de la Boétie.

p. 37 **Farewell to my Fancy.** My friend John Bosley was for some time the exemplary churchwarden of our Anglican community in Los Gigantes, Tenerife. His wife Katherine succeeded him in office and was even more exemplary. This affectionate but shamelessly flirtateous poem does less than justice to her awesome administrative competence.

p. 38   **The Old Spagnoletta**   This is the name of a dance tune by Elizabethan composer Giles Fanaby (ca. 1560--ca. 1620). It is 6/4 time, in dotted rhythms imitating, perhaps, the steps of a dance, which I do not try to follow here, imitating only the general vigour of the tune.

p. 44 **Reflections**   The "little river" is the Soar, in Leicestershire, where I used to own a house on the river bank.

Lines 20-21 "placidly reaffirms strong presences", ie. literally, of trees reflected in the water, and figuratively, of friends clearly remembered.

Late News

i. Change and Decay

p. 53 **Beach Resort**   The poem presents the changing states of the tide, moon-drawn, in the course of one day, as an image of changing states and aspirations in life.

Line 3 "abs and pecs", abdominal and pectoral muscles.

Line 11   "cable stitch" Dictionaries assert, in various wordings, the resemblance of this knitting pattern to twisted ropes. More relevant here is the use of cable stitch in sports gear, particularly cricket pullovers.

Line 13--14 "a tennis court (short)": "short tennis", a variety of the game adapted for children.

Line 17 "ball" — as in "game", also as in "dance".

Line 23 "takes a minute": minute as in "sixty seconds", and as "a note of business proceedings".

Line 24   "closure"= a) "conclusion" b) "shut down" (of a business)

p. 54 **One Deaf Poet**   This is the most recent version of this poem. I am not altogether deaf, but badly "hearing impaired", with hearing aids that I often prefer to go without when I am alone, and do not need when I am writing.

Line 21 "Spooner" The Revd. W A Spooner (1844-1920) of New College, Oxford, and Headmaster of Oswestry School, known for his unintentional transposing of word-initial sounds, as in "Is the bean dizzy?" for "Is the Dean busy ?" "You have tasted two worms." for "You have wasted two terms" etc. "Wonderland" evokes the word-wrangling of Alice's companions at their tea-party (*Alice's Adventure in Wonderland,* chapter 7) eg. The Hatter's "you might just as well say that 'I see what I eat' is the same as 'I eat what I see!"

p. 55 *Poem in Old Age*

Line 28 "creature fantasies"= "pleasurable fancies", cp. "creature comforts".

Line 30 "ignoring the raven": not the raven in the Hatter's riddle, but the bird that croaks "Nevermore" in Edgar Allan Poe's poem *The Raven.*

p. 56 *So Long at the Clinic*   This poem, about the longueurs of attending a N H S clinic, is an extended villanelle (see the note, above, on **The Fall of Man**). Instead of 19 lines, it has 22 (not at first intentionally but eventually deliberate, reflecting the length of the "waiting bit").

p. 57 *Lost Objects*

Line 6 "dim Platonic void"= "merely speculative existence".

Line 21 "picayaune"= "trivial, petty". The usage is North American rather than British, the linguistic background French/Canadian and Hispanic

ii Getting and Spending

p. 60 *Instant Access*

Line 16 "quiz the Hesperides": in one of its various meanings, "Hesperides" refers to the "Islands of the Blest" in the western sea, beyond the last pitch of land, where heroes and holymen were said to go to their reward after virtuous lives. Most loosely interpreted it might signify the Canary Islands, off the coast of Morocco, which Britons visit periodically in pursuit of organised pleasure.

p. 61 **Makeover**   "Makeover" is a noun, comprising one of the senses of "make over", a phrasal verb as defined by Collins English Dictionary 1. to transfer the title or possession of (property etc) 2. to renovate, or remodel. Collins adds, in definition of the noun 'makeover', "a complete remodelling". This was the title, and the effect, of a British television programme in which neighbours were invited to collude in the making over of rooms in each other's houses.

Line 24 "a foolish move": "move" as in house, also "move" as in chess etc. Similarly line 25, "on the wrong premises", punning on "premises" as location and "premise" as phillosophical position.

p. 63   **We Pin-ball Machines.**   Here is a metaphysical "conceit": that human beings, purporting to exercise free will in their pursuit of happiness, are like pin-ball machines affecting control of their chances and painted scenarios.

Line 12 "hopalong lariat": a cowboy-figure's whirling lasso ("lariat" from Spanish *la reata*, "the rope"); "hopalong" is a transferred epithet, borrowed from the name of the virtuous cowboy Hopalong Cassidy, played in films in the 1930's and 40's by the revered actor William Boyd (1895-1972)

p. 64   **Phantoms of the Opera**   But the reference is not to the Gothic novel by Gaston Leroux (1868--1927), brought to the musical stage (1986) by Andrew Lloyd Webber, rather to the splendid *opera bouffe, Le Nozze di Figaro* (1786), scripted by the witty Lorenzo da Ponte (1749--1838) to the music of the immortal Wolfgang Amadeus Mozart (1756-1791).

Line 9 *epicene* : "having characteristic of both sexes", or "sexless".

Lines 19--20 "survival by playing the game and the rules". Figaro, faced with defeat by his opponents, escapes on technical points.

Line 37.   *the grace of Amadeus*   Mozart's baptismal name, Gottlieb, latinised as "Amadeus", "God's love", or "beloved of God". *Amadeo* was a quite common name in Italy in the early middle ages.

p. 65   **Below the Stockbroker Belt**   A two-in-one title, combining "Stockbroker Belt", an area where prosperous stockbrokers live, and "below the belt", a low blow in boxing.

p. 66   **Selby**   A poem with a theme in treatment and a larger theme in view. the theme in treatment is the cruel existence of feral cats, an "outsider" species, in Tenerife. The theme in view is the fate of an "outsider" human species, the old and infirm.

Lines 1 and 2 refer to a massive deep-mining coalfield around Selby in the Vale of Selby, officially opened in 1976, finally closed down as "uneconomic" in 2004.

Line 5   "sell-by date":   the instruction printed on packages of perishable goods and foodstuffs.

Line 42   "stifled by the State": not "killed", but "minimally provided for".

iii Political Animals

p. 70   **Portrait of a Statesman**   Devised in imitation of the popular rhetoric and vocal mannerisms of a ministerial person who retired from office in 2007.

p. 71   **Speaking of Herod**

Line 3   P R: Public Relations. "showmanshite", in cloacal mimicry of "showmanship".

Line 6   "pancake", a heavy cosmetic base of make-up.

Lines 7--8   "to be a sight to frighten........Israel": parody of the Nunc Dimittis, "to be a light to lighten the Gentiles and to be the glory of thy people Israel."

Line 17 "the slap of firm government", political cant phrase of, I think, American origin, the quasi-parental discipline of an electorate for its own good."

Lines 20--21 "peering out.......peering in", parodic rephrasing of what Lyndon B Johnson said to Edgar Hoover. "it's probably better to have him inside the tent peeing out, than outside peeing in", the tent being the structure of government.

p. 72   *Them Batrachians*   "The frog people"

Line 11 "flooding this country, taking homes, jobs"; the common accusation against *hoi batrachoi*, bearing no correspondence with statistical fact.

Line 19 "and I, coward, drink my tea"; our encounter is at a roadside kiosk.

p. 73   *Elections*   This poem was written at the time of the American elections, dominated by Barack Obama's candidacy.

Line 18 "the Enlightenment": in general, the optimistic 18th century.

Lines 26 ff "our candidates face trial by vilification and then emerge all squeaky-clean in staybright suits to explain themselves to the Press" : my impression of an almost oppressively painstaking, complete, agonisingly just electoral system.

p. 74   *The Old Aluminium Faces*   Possibly the oldest poem in this collection, written, I think, during Harold Wilson's premiership (1964--70). The political rhetoric (the taxpayers' money etc) is still familiar and only a detail or two has an old-fashioned ring — eg. the Range Rover of line 20 would now bear a different name for luxury.

Line 24   "kip in cardboard......": the homeless slept in shop doorways or other recesses, in cardboard wrappings, or under sheets of cardboard — until woken and moved on by the police.

p. 75   *Turnabout*   This is an imitation, on current political terms, of an anonymous poem from the early 17th century. *The Old and Young Courtier* I find the text of the latter in Richard Aldington (ed) *Poetry of the English -Speaking World* (William Heinemann, London and Toronto 1947). It is readily accessible online through http://www.telelib.com My text, a modern satire, merely "shadows" this original. "Turnabout" is the periodic revolution of dominant political parties.

Line 32   "a ready-made hand for the three-card trick": sometimes called "find the lady" (ie. queen of hearts or diamonds) This is a street trickster's easy method of getting money out of the gullible.

Line 35   "takeaway" : as in "take away food", but also "take away" as in deduct (levy, tax)

Line 40   "fresh-thinking Faker": the need of fresh thinking was one of the urgent aspirations of the New Labour party in its early days.

Line 41   "neb": northern dialect for "nose" (and also the peak of a cap).
          "tyke": a mongrel dog (and also a Yorkshireman).

p. 77   **Caesar is Coming**   Note: In A D 9 the German chieftain Arminius was blocking imperial expansion east of the Rhine. An armed force of three legions, sent to keep order in the province, was enmeshed and massacred in a tract called the Teutoburger Forest. Some seven years later, in A D 16, Germanicus Caesar conducted a punitive campaign, devastating but ultimately inconclusive, across the Rhine frontier.

p. 78 *A Sense of Compromise*   The familiar (indeed hackneyed) setting and characters of a Western film point to a shocking moral conclusion.

Line 4 "rantipole": OED   1. Noun "a wild, disorderly, reckless person".
                       2. Adjective "wild, reckless, disorderly"

This fits the meaning, but I confess to being taken by the mere sound of the word, which seemed to fit the triple skip of the polka.

Line 12   "two aces and a regal pair"   I am not a poker player; my only assumption about this "hand" is that "his leathership" has come by it dishonestly.

Line 20   "broads": professional ladies

Line 26   "brilliantine": a hair cream, no longer much, if at all, in use by stylish men.

Line 29   "between the brackets of his beastly frown" ie. between the eyes.

Line 34   *missa est*: the *ite, missa est* that dismisses the congregation at the close of the Roman mass.

Lines 41--48: the disturbing "immoral" conclusion is that in our dreams, or the life of the subconscious, we regularly subvert the moral teachings of consciousness; ie. (surprise) that we are born sinners.

iv Night Thoughts

p. 82   Early Evening TV

Line 22   "the footballer bought for a cool two million bucks", ie. footballer in the round-ball code. They do not come as cheap in 2009. The latest top price is eighty million pounds. I refrain from moral comment, but imply it.

p. 83 All Hallows   "All Hallows"=All Saints.
All Saints Eve, 31st October, Hallowe'en, when kind spirits walk again in their earthly haunts. Known to wayward children as "Mischief Night", in America as "Trick or Treat ?"

p. 84 Cold Starlight

Line 23 quotes St John who says that in the beginning was the *logos*. The *logos* is the first principle, the prime mover, which St John then identifies with God.

Line 26-27 "the light that laves the sky's uttermost seaborne rim": this thin band of horizon light is commonly observable in westward prospect, the last of sundown.

Lines 29-30 "What is man, that thou art mindful of him.........? Psalm 8:4.

p. 87 **What Comes Next**

Line 5 "the relentless Kalends": the ruthless passage of time. In Roman chronology, the Kalends were the first days of the month (whence, of course, "calendar")
Line 5 "takeaway" man, punning on "take away" as deprive and takeaway as in American, "food to go".

Line 17 "if I get to the place". I had first written "when I get to the place", but changed it. I am not a Calvinist, but "if" seemed, somehow, less presumptuous.

Epilogue

p. 90 **On the Go**

Lines 29--31 names moments in the Eucharist (or Mass) "I believe", "Our Father", "Glory be to God on high". Never mind the labels, just keep taking the pills.

p. 92 **Nocturnal** Quoted here from Ecclesiastes 12:4 "and the doors shall be shut in the streets"......"and all the daughters of song shall be brought low".

p. 93 **Postscript from the Hesperides**

Line 25 "Celebs" ie. celebrities, not quite the same as people of merit and talent.

Line 26 "helots" a class of serfs in ancient Sparta at feasts brought in and made drunk for the amusement of their social superiors.

Line 27   "tribunes of the plebs" in lawmaking status, but holding the power of veto.

Line 38   "If England were what England seems" quotes Kipling's poem, *The Return:*
> If England were what England seems
> An' not the England of our dreams
> But only putty, brass an' paint,
> 'Ow soon we'd drop her. But she ain't.

Line 62   "avatars"   I take one of the definitions of *avatar* in Webster's New World Dictionary, 2nd College edition (1984) "any incarnation of embodiment, as of a concept in a person".

Line 76--77   "great rocks towering a thousand feet above the foam". The rocks are the huge cliffs of the Acantilado de los Gigantes, "the coast of the giants," towering a thousand feet above the end of the street where I now live.

*   *   *   *   *   *

Forthcoming publications:

The Seed Bed— Four English Writers

Health and Healing
(Poems in Polish and English)

Beyond the Cloister Publications
74 Marina St Leonards-on-Sea TN 38 0BJ
beyondcloister@hotmail.co.uk
www.beyondthecloister